D0793749

DOLPHINS SET I

BOTTLENOSE DOLPHINS

Megan M. Gunderson
ABDO Publishing Company

visit us at
www.abdopublishing.com

Published by ABDO Publishing Company, 8000 West 78th Street, Edina, Minnesota 55439.
Copyright © 2011 by Abdo Consulting Group, Inc. International copyrights reserved in all
countries. No part of this book may be reproduced in any form without written permission
from the publisher. The Checkerboard Library™ is a trademark and logo of ABDO
Publishing Company.

Printed in the United States of America, North Mankato, Minnesota.
042010
092010

 PRINTED ON RECYCLED PAPER

Cover Photo: Corbis
Interior Photos: Alamy pp. 5, 17; © Doug Perrine / SeaPics.com pp. 12–13, 14;
    iStockphoto p. 15; National Geographic Stock p. 8; Peter Arnold pp. 19, 21;
    Uko Gorter pp. 7, 9

Editor: Heidi M.D. Elston
Art Direction & Cover Design: Neil Klinepier

Library of Congress Cataloging-in-Publication Data

Gunderson, Megan M., 1981-
  Bottlenose dolphins / Megan M. Gunderson.
      p. cm. -- (Dolphins)
  Includes index.
  ISBN 978-1-61613-411-2
  1. Bottlenose dolphin--Juvenile literature. I. Title.
  QL737.C432G857 2010
  599.53--dc22
                                        2010001623

CONTENTS

BOTTLENOSE DOLPHINS 4

SIZE, SHAPE, AND COLOR 6

WHERE THEY LIVE 8

SENSES 10

DEFENSE 12

FOOD 14

BABIES 16

BEHAVIORS 18

BOTTLENOSE DOLPHIN FACTS . . . 20

GLOSSARY 22

WEB SITES 23

INDEX 24

BOTTLENOSE DOLPHINS

Bottlenose dolphins are popular animals that are often seen in zoos and aquariums. Their mouths curve up so they are always smiling. These dolphins rank among the world's most intelligent animals.

Bottlenose dolphins are **cetaceans** that belong to the family **Delphinidae**. There are two bottlenose dolphin species. These are the common bottlenose dolphin and the Indo-Pacific bottlenose dolphin.

Like all cetaceans, bottlenose dolphins are mammals. That means they are **warm-blooded** and nurse their young with milk. Bottlenose dolphins have lungs and breathe air above water. They draw in air through a blowhole located at the top of the head.

Indo-Pacific and common bottlenose dolphins (below) were once considered a single species.

SIZE, SHAPE, AND COLOR

Bottlenose dolphins grow 6 to 13 feet (1.8 to 4 m) long. On average, they weigh 330 to 440 pounds (150 to 200 kg). Yet, some weigh more than twice that! Common bottlenose dolphins are generally larger than Indo-Pacific bottlenose dolphins. In both species, females are usually smaller than males.

The bottlenose dolphin's tall, pointed dorsal fin curves backward. The dolphin uses its flukes to swim and its pointed flippers to steer. The Indo-Pacific bottlenose has a more slender beak than the common bottlenose dolphin.

The bottlenose dolphin has smooth, rubbery skin. The sides of its body are light gray, while its back is

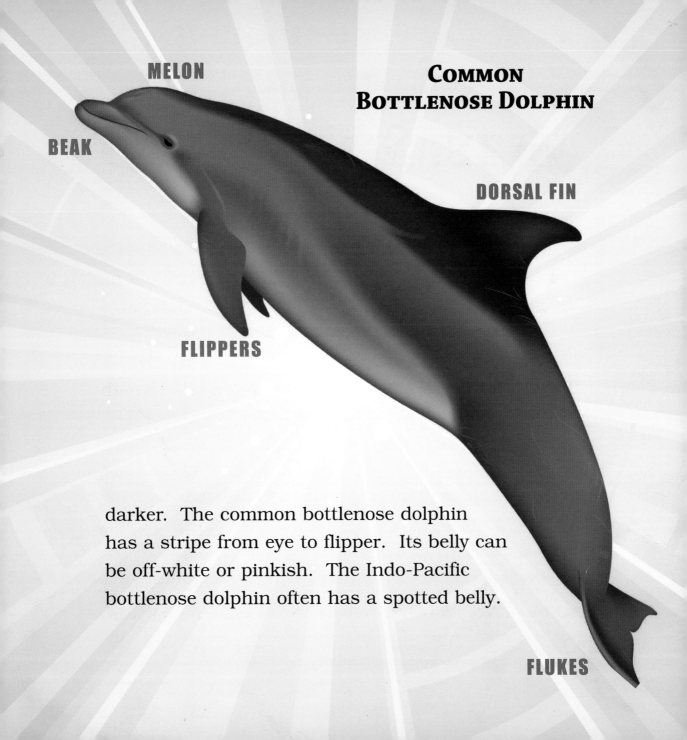

MELON

BEAK

COMMON
BOTTLENOSE DOLPHIN

DORSAL FIN

FLIPPERS

darker. The common bottlenose dolphin
has a stripe from eye to flipper. Its belly can
be off-white or pinkish. The Indo-Pacific
bottlenose dolphin often has a spotted belly.

FLUKES

WHERE THEY LIVE

Common bottlenose dolphins are found all over the world except in the polar seas. They prefer **tropical** and **temperate** waters. These include parts of the Atlantic, Indian, and Pacific oceans. They also swim in the Black and Mediterranean seas.

Many bottlenose dolphins live around islands, including the Hawaiian Islands.

Some common bottlenose dolphins live offshore, while others live near the coast. They also travel into bays, **estuaries**, and the ends of rivers.

Indo-Pacific bottlenose dolphins prefer tropical and **subtropical** waters. They are found along coasts in

Where Do Bottlenose Dolphins Live?

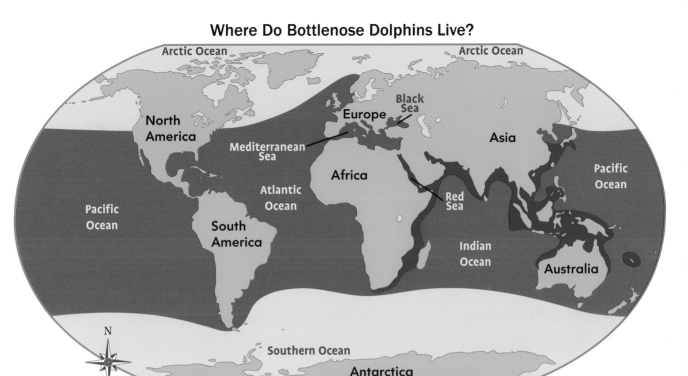

common bottlenose dolphins   Indo-Pacific bottlenose dolphins

the Indian and western Pacific oceans. They also live in the Red Sea. Sometimes, common bottlenose dolphins share their range.

Some bottlenose dolphins **migrate** seasonally. They might follow moving food sources or changing water temperatures.

SENSES

To navigate its underwater world, the bottlenose dolphin relies on its excellent senses. Its keen sense of hearing tells the dolphin exactly where a sound is coming from.

Hearing is also important for echolocation. The dolphin sends out a series of clicks through its **melon**. These hit underwater objects and bounce back for the dolphin to hear. The returning echoes tell it the size, distance, and speed of the objects. Echolocation helps the dolphin identify food sources and enemies.

The dolphin's eyes move independently. Its eyesight is good in and out of water and in low light. Touch is an important sense for feeling objects and socializing. The skin is especially sensitive around the blowhole, the eyes, and the mouth.

Scientists believe bottlenose dolphins may lack a sense of smell. However, bottlenose dolphins do have a sense of taste. They prefer certain foods over others.

Sound wave sent out by dolphin

Echo wave received by dolphin

DEFENSE

Bottlenose dolphins have several natural enemies. They include great white, tiger, dusky, bull, and mako sharks. Killer whales attack bottlenose dolphins, too. Fishing nets, pollution, boat traffic, and disease are additional threats.

Swimming away is one defense bottlenose dolphins have. They can

Many dolphins have scars or bite marks from shark attacks.

travel 18 to 22 miles per hour (29 to 35 km/h) for short bursts.

Bottlenose dolphins will also work together to fight off a predator. Afterward, they may even aid an injured dolphin. Bottlenose dolphins have helped

other dolphins to the surface to breathe.

A bottlenose dolphin's coloring is another defense. The light belly helps it blend in when seen from below. When seen from above, the dark back hides it against dark, deep water.

FOOD

Bottlenose dolphins often work as a group to hunt their food. They enjoy squid, shrimps, and a variety of fish.

Coastal dolphins chase fish into shallow water or even onto **mudflats**. To get the food, the dolphins must partially **beach** themselves. Offshore, dolphins will herd prey into a cluster. Then, they take turns charging in to feed.

Bottlenose dolphins also catch food using a method called

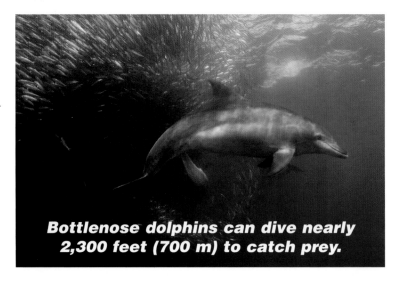

Bottlenose dolphins can dive nearly 2,300 feet (700 m) to catch prey.

fish whacking. They use their flukes to strike fish and knock them right out of the water! This stuns the prey so the dolphins can catch it.

Bottlenose dolphins use their teeth to grasp their prey, not to chew it. Common bottlenose dolphins have up to 100 sharp, cone-shaped teeth. An Indo-Pacific bottlenose dolphin's jaws hold up to 116 teeth!

If the prey is large, the dolphin shakes it or rubs it on the ocean floor. This breaks the food into smaller pieces the dolphin can swallow.

BABIES

Bottlenose dolphins may mate at any time of year. Afterward, a female bottlenose dolphin is **pregnant** for about 12 months. She usually gives birth to a single baby dolphin, or calf.

At birth, a common bottlenose calf measures up to 55 inches (140 cm). It weighs up to 44 pounds (20 kg). A newborn Indo-Pacific bottlenose calf can be 44 inches (112 cm) long. It weighs up to 46 pounds (21 kg).

An adult male rarely helps raise his calf. Often, a mother and her calf will spend time in a group of related females.

Like other mammals, the mother dolphin provides milk for her calf. Common bottlenose calves nurse for 18 to 24 months. Indo-Pacific bottlenose calves nurse for 18 to 20 months.

Most bottlenose dolphins can reach more than 40 years of age. Female common bottlenose dolphins can live more than 50 years.

A bottlenose calf stays with its mother for at least three years.

BEHAVIORS

Bottlenose dolphins swim in groups. Near shore, they form groups of 2 to 15 dolphins. Offshore, groups can have hundreds of members!

Bottlenose dolphins have also been seen swimming with other **cetaceans**. These include pilot whales, Risso's dolphins, spotted dolphins, and rough-toothed dolphins.

To communicate with group members, bottlenose dolphins slap their flukes on the water. They also use clicks and whistles. Each bottlenose dolphin creates its own whistle. Scientists use these sounds to identify individual dolphins. Calves use them to find their mothers.

Bottlenose dolphins enjoy swimming in the waves created in front of ships.

Bottlenose dolphins enjoy playing in the water. These impressive jumpers can leap up to 16 feet (5 m) out of the water! They also love riding waves. These entertaining animals are always fun to watch!

Bottlenose Dolphin Facts

Scientific Name:

Common bottlenose dolphin *Tursiops truncatus*

Indo-Pacific bottlenose dolphin *Tursiops aduncus*

Common Names:

Common bottlenose dolphin

Indo-Pacific bottlenose dolphin

Average Size: Bottlenose dolphins grow 6 to 13 feet (1.8 to 4 m) in length. On average, they weigh 330 to 440 pounds (150 to 200 kg).

Where They're Found: In the Atlantic, Pacific, and Indian oceans and the Mediterranean, Black, and Red seas

Glossary

beach - to strand on a beach.

cetacean (sih-TAY-shuhn) - a member of the order Cetacea. Mammals such as dolphins, whales, and porpoises are cetaceans.

Delphinidae (dehl-FIHN-uh-dee) - the scientific name for the oceanic dolphin family. It includes dolphins that live mostly in salt water.

estuary (EHS-chuh-wehr-ee) - the area of water where a river's current meets an ocean's tide.

melon - a rounded structure found in the forehead of some cetaceans.

migrate - to move from one place to another, often to find food.

mudflat - a level area of land usually lying just below the water's surface.

pregnant - having one or more babies growing within the body.

subtropical - relating to an area where average temperatures range between 55 and 68 degrees Fahrenheit (13 and 20°C).

temperate - relating to an area where average temperatures range between 50 and 55 degrees Fahrenheit (10 and 13°C).

tropical - relating to an area with an average temperature above 77 degrees Fahrenheit (25°C) where no freezing occurs.

warm-blooded - having a body temperature that is not much affected by surrounding air or water.

WEB SITES

To learn more about bottlenose dolphins, visit ABDO Publishing Company on the World Wide Web at **www.abdopublishing.com**. Web sites about bottlenose dolphins are featured on our Book Links page. These links are routinely monitored and updated to provide the most current information available.

INDEX

A

Atlantic Ocean 8

B

beak 6
Black Sea 8
blowhole 4, 10

C

calves 4, 16, 18
color 6, 7, 13
communication 18

D

defense 12, 13
Delphinidae (family)
    4
dorsal fin 6

E

echolocation 10
eyes 7, 10

F

flippers 6, 7
flukes 6, 15, 18
food 4, 9, 10, 11,
    14, 15, 16

G

groups 14, 16, 18

H

habitat 8, 9, 14,
    15, 18
hunting 14, 15

I

Indian Ocean 8, 9

L

leaping 19
life span 17

M

mammals 4, 16
Mediterranean Sea
    8
melon 10
migration 9
mouth 4, 10

P

Pacific Ocean 8, 9

R

Red Sea 9
reproduction 16

S

senses 10, 11
size 6, 16
skin 6, 10
speed 13

T

teeth 15
threats 10, 12, 13